YOUR KNOWLEDGE HAS VALUE

- We will publish your bachelor's and master's thesis, essays and papers

- Your own eBook and book - sold worldwide in all relevant shops

- Earn money with each sale

Upload your text at www.GRIN.com and publish for free

Bibliographic information published by the German National Library:

The German National Library lists this publication in the National Bibliography; detailed bibliographic data are available on the Internet at http://dnb.dnb.de .

Imprint:

Copyright © 2008 GRIN Verlag, Open Publishing GmbH
Print and binding: Books on Demand GmbH, Norderstedt Germany
ISBN: 9783640453535

This book at GRIN:

http://www.grin.com/en/e-book/137331/migration-in-germany-violent-crimes-committed-by-young-men-of-foreign

Sandro Sterneberg

Migration in Germany - Violent crimes committed by young men of foreign orignis

GRIN Publishing

GRIN - Your knowledge has value

Since its foundation in 1998, GRIN has specialized in publishing academic texts by students, college teachers and other academics as e-book and printed book. The website www.grin.com is an ideal platform for presenting term papers, final papers, scientific essays, dissertations and specialist books.

Visit us on the internet:

http://www.grin.com/

http://www.facebook.com/grincom

http://www.twitter.com/grin_com

– Essay –

Topic:

Migration in Germany:
Violent crimes committed by young men of foreign orignis

Author:

Sandro Sterneberg

Course:

Political Economy and Social Structures
of Modern Societies
Berlin School of Economics
Winter semester 2007/2008

Table of contents:

1. Violent crimes committed by young men of foreign origins

In the 1960s the Federal Republic of Germany signed contracts with Turkey and other countries to send workers, mostly from rural areas, to support the booming industrial economy (The German Economic Miracle). It was clear for the German government and the foreign workers that they would stay only for a limited time. Because companies needed the so called "Gastarbeiter" frequently for a fairly long time, limited work visas were extended or even turned into unlimited permissions. Nevertheless there was not really the intention by the German governments to integrate them into the society neither there was a real intention by the foreigners to integrate themselves. Later many of them left the country but a lot of especially Turkish people chose to stay. After the reunification with the German Democratic Republic in 1991 and in the following years the economical situation for low-skilled workers became worse. A large part of industrial production was shifted abroad, there was a surplus of men power and the new emerged service sector could not compensate it. Due to wars also massive waves of refugees from e.g. former Yugoslavian countries as well as Arabian countries like Lebanon and Palestine arrived Germany. [1][2]

Nowadays, as discussed in the course Political Economy and Social Structures of Modern Societies at the Berlin School of Economics in the winter semester 2007/ 2008, Germany is a country of immigration which faces the challenges but also chances of a multicultural society. Unfortunately many foreign families are dependent on public transfer payments and therefore in poor social and economical situations because the often low-skilled heads of the family do not have jobs or are for legal reasons not allowed to work. People who are living under difficult conditions with no prospect for a positive change are likely to become criminals. Especially male teenagers and young men with migrant backgrounds (between 14-25 years) are in larger German cities more likely to be intensive culprits and commit robberies, dangerous/ hard body violence, sexual abuses as well as rapes than their German counterparts. Furthermore a number of unrecorded cases exists because it is known that there is a different behavior in reporting crimes by Germans than by strangers. Besides there is no statistical differentiation between native Germans and foreigners who were admitted to citizenship which means that the figures are probably much higher and alarming. [3]

Therefore juvenile delinquency is an important issue for Germany which has been discussed in the public dispute for many years. The scandal about the "Rütli-Hauptschule" in Berlin (2006), where tutors refused to give lessons because they felt threatened by pupils, was probably just the tip of the iceberg but led together with other scandals again to a debate to find solutions for this problem. [4]

During the election campaign in the Bundesland (Federal State) Hessen Roland Koch, politician of the German Christian Democratic Party, named a resolution. He proposed that young criminals, so particularly young males with migrant backgrounds, should be more severe punished. Young criminals between 18-21 years should be treated like adults, the maximum prison sentence for young

[1] cf. Landeskommission Berlin gegen Gewalt (2007), p. 14
[2] cf. Landeskommission Berlin gegen Gewalt (2007), p. 83-88
[3] cf. Landeskommission Berlin gegen Gewalt (2007), p. 19-23
[4] cf. Süddeutsche (2007)

people should be increased from 10 to 15 years and it should be possible to deport foreigners from Germany if they were sentenced to a one year imprisonment. [5] [6]

Although it perhaps was a statement to catch votes during the election campaign even so it could be a solution for the problem. But is this the only and above all the best solution? The author of this essay has been following the discussion and was beside solution interested in having a look behind the various reasons for their bearing to get committed to crimes. For that Berlin, the capital of Germany, was a very good example because it is one of the most cultural diverse cities in Germany and has got a high crime rate among young males with foreign origins. In addition the "Landeskommission Berlin gegen Gewalt" assigned between 2005 and 2007 a task force consisting of scientists, members of the police, public services and representatives of migrant organizations to examine the issue in detail as well as to work out recommendations for a possible solution. [7]

The aim of this essay is to state reasons for their behavior and to compare the suggestion by Roland Koch with the suggestions of the task force for an improvement in the situation.

2. Reasons for violent behavior by young men of foreign origins

Berlin is one of the most culturally diverse cities in Germany and has a high youth crime rate. Teenagers and young adults with Turkish, Kurdish, Lebanese, former Yugoslavian and unknown or unsure (often Palestinian) nationalities are much more likely to be criminals than their German counterparts. [8] Although young women are often in similar social and economical situations they are not as often as young men committed to violent crimes. This leads to the questions why especially young males with migrant backgrounds become culprits. [9] Cultural, social, economical, legal status caused and personal factors can be taken into consideration for their more aggressive and violent behavior.

First of all the puberty can be a difficult period for all male teenagers because their bodies are often developing much faster than they are maturing mentally. During this time they also try out various things to find out who they are. It is for example often ordinary for boys to measure their strengths by doing sport activities and competitions but also by brawls among themselves. Compared to German especially foreign teenagers are more likely to exaggerate this and also to use violence instead of verbal discussions to solve conflicts in general.

One reason for this may be the traditional role model in their cultural and/ or religious circles. Even nowadays their communities often expect men to be dominant, to care for the maintenance of their families and to protect them (also by using violence if necessary) against others. In contrary women are expected to obey men as well as to take care of the children and the household. In accordance to this parents educate boys and girls differently to prepare them for their future roles within the family. Whereas boys are frequent allowed to do almost everything they want, girls have a lot of household duties and not as many privileges as boys. As mentioned before women should frequently obey men and

---

[5] cf. Spiegel Online (2008a)
[6] cf. Spiegel Online (2008b)
[7] cf. Landeskommission Berlin gegen Gewalt (2007), p. 8-11
[8] cf. Landeskommission Berlin gegen Gewalt (2007), p. 19-23
[9] cf. Landeskommission Berlin gegen Gewalt (2007), p. 24-27

if they don't it is sometimes also legitimated that men force them by threatening to beat them and even to do it. If men within a family beat women (the mother, female children or other female relatives) to carry through their will, young males learn very early that they can assert themselves against others and particularly women by using violence. On the other hand it could also be the case that they were beaten within the family and that they experience violence as a normal form of nonverbal communication.

In other words it is possible that violence is, within their circles and/ or families, not as seen as such a bad thing. Violent behavior may also be sometimes necessary to express dominance, masculinity, the ability to protect a family and therefore to correspond to their traditional role-model. [10] [11] [12]

Even though this common used stereotype of a lively and aggressive southerner macho might still exist, it is not a proper explanation because there are must be other factors while some of them behave violent and some not. It can be said that in a tendency a lot of the former Gastarbeiter were low-skilled, low-educated and had a low knowledge of the German language. When there were enough jobs for these kind of people they were able to take care of the maintenance of their families. It was also often no need to get higher education and to improve their language skills so that their education level remained nearly the same. As mentioned in the introduction, times have changed. Nowadays there are not as many jobs for low-skilled worker as there were in the past and this can be among other things a reason why many former foreign workers are unemployed in these days. Owing to the low-education-level and insufficient language skills of their parents also the children are likely to have similar problems. As a result around 55% of pupils with migrant backgrounds have language problems. [13]

Another problem is that foreign families are often strongly connected with their cultural/ religious communities and that they are socially segregated which means that they often stay in districts with many other foreigners and just a few Germans. Because of this the parents and their children have big difficulties to learn the language and to integrate into the society because they may still be integrated in parallel societies in which it is not always necessary to speak German. Inadequate language skills can lead to bad school results, block access to higher education and limit job prospects. [14]

Although the "Allgemeines Gleichbehandlungsgesetz" was passed in 2006 there may also be still a structural discrimination in kindergartens, schools, universities, on the labour market as well as during leisure time. A lot of foreigners might experienced that other pupils got better marks although their results were quite similar and that teachers do not properly support children with language problems. Furthermore they might experienced that their families did not get the desired accommodation, that they were refused to enter night clubs, that they did not get the chance to serve apprenticeships or to show their capacities by carrying out a job because they are foreigners. [15]

---

[10] cf. Landeskommission Berlin gegen Gewalt (2007), p. 12-18
[11] cf. Landeskommission Berlin gegen Gewalt (2007), p. 37-49
[12] cf. Landeskommission Berlin gegen Gewalt (2007), p. 24-27
[13] cf. Landeskommission Berlin gegen Gewalt (2007), p. 28-36
[14] cf. Landeskommission Berlin gegen Gewalt (2007), p. 50-55
[15] cf. Landeskommission Berlin gegen Gewalt (2007), p. 55-56

Due to their legal status especially refugees from the former Yugoslavian countries, Lebanon and Palestine have frequently permissions to stay but not to work. Without earning money by themselves and being independent from public transfer payments it is hard to take care of the living of their families and their prospects for a positive change are bad. Besides referring to their legal status foreigners who have been living in Germany for a fairly long time are for example also not allowed to vote and can therefore not equally participate in society as Germans can do. [16] [17]

To summarize it may be possible that violence for solving conflicts is legitimated by their cultural/ religious communities and that they therefore, if necessary, use this instrument to carry through their will. On the other hand many young males are especially because of traditional role models under a big pressure. Although they can not take their fathers as good examples because they are often low-educated, can not support their sons as well as unemployed and not able to feed their families, they nevertheless should correspond to the role model. In addition young foreign females are referring to the role model more used to get conform with their environment. This results in better language skills, better school results and therefore better job perspectives as their male counterparts. So young foreign men are frustrated because they experience that their job prospects are worse compared to those of young German males and even foreign females. They also feel discriminated as well as strangers in the German society and the last lingering way to demonstrate strength, superiority, dominance and therefore masculinity is violent behavior.

3. Recommendations for an improvement in the situation

As mentioned before foreign families and therefore also their children often live under bad social and economical conditions. They often do not properly speak German and do not have jobs. Furthermore they feel discriminated and not accepted in the German society because their job prospects are often worse than Germans or they are because of legal reasons not allowed to work. Furthermore they are socially segregated because they stay in districts with a low rate of German inhabitants and/ or choose to live in their cultural communities and therefore quasi in parallel societies. As a result of an unsure future as well as no real prospect for a positive change especially young males are committed to crimes to improve their economical situation or to express their feeling of hopelessness and frustration. To improve the situation or to solve the problem of juvenile delinquency completely the task force named different recommendations concerning kindergartens, schools, youth offices (agencies responsible for education and welfare of young people), police, judiciaries, legal status, labour market and migrant organisations.

First of all kindergartens should be free of charge so that migrant families are much more encouraged to take their children to these institutions. All in all the kindergartens should also become much more than today institutions for education and learning. To achieve this goal it is necessary that teachers are better educated regarding intercultural competencies, get a higher payment and that their work is higher granted because it is so important for the children. Today nearly 50% of

---

[16] cf. Landeskommission Berlin gegen Gewalt (2007), p. 34-36
[17] cf. Landeskommission Berlin gegen Gewalt (2007), p. 56-62

the children have a migrant background and because of this it is essential to employ more male and also more teacher with foreign origins. That might be more successful because boys (referring to the role model) often respect the authority of male teachers rather than female teachers and foreign educators could better understand their special needs. Besides parents should be more participated. Referring to their language problems this could be reached by holding up multi-lingual information events and generally by having personal development talks for all of the children. [18]

Regarding the schools the task force recommended to provide knowledge but also to focus more on the development of personal and social competencies. There should also be more support for pupils with difficulties in general and particularly with language problems. Furthermore there should be less "Hauptschulen" (low-qualifying degree) and more full-time-schools (at least the opportunity to obtain a higher-qualifying degree) as well as an expanded offer of activities like theatre, music, dancing, various sports conceivable in cooperation with sport / cultural associations. This could improve the social segregation and improve their feeling of non-being-accepted as well as their chances to higher education. Due to the high rate of foreign pupils it also makes sense to discuss in class religious, cultural and gender diversity, the German law system and in the bargain violence. As recommended for the kindergartens it is also advisable for schools to participate parents in another way so that they are more bind to the school and could accompany their children more successfully. To put all of these things into effect a higher amount of teachers and psychologists as well as a higher esteem of their work by the society is essential. [19, 20]

So that youth offices are able to supervise particularly intensive culprits and their parents, they need more and better educated staff in general as well as more staff with foreign origins. Another suggestion is to sanction parents who do not adequately fulfil their duties by for e.g. reducing transfer payments. [21]

Also the police should change their kind of view. It is for example a problem that young Turkish men often do not respect the authority of policemen in Germany because policemen in Turkey fit into a different role model. These Policemen rather act as big brothers, uncles or old men who have to be respected whereas the authority of the German police relies on power given by the state. To understand young foreign men and their situations policemen should get more intercultural trainings. Due to this it would also be good if there would be more policemen with migrant backgrounds. Another aspect is that there should be a closer cooperation between police and youth offices. So youth offices are better informed about crimes and able to take actions earlier, it would help if data of culprits would be much more transmitted to them. Furthermore there should be more questioning of accused together with their parents so that there is also a closer contact between police and parents. [22]

Besides it would be sensible if there would be a closer cooperation between the judiciaries, schools and youth offices. This could for example mean that the judiciaries react faster to crimes and transmit data of culprits to schools and youth offices so that they are well instructed and can possibly prevent further crimes.

---

[18] cf. Landeskommission Berlin gegen Gewalt (2007), p. 168-171
[19] cf. Landeskommission Berlin gegen Gewalt (2007), p. 171-181
[20] cf. Landeskommission Berlin gegen Gewalt (2007), p. 189-192
[21] cf. Landeskommission Berlin gegen Gewalt (2007), p. 181-189
[22] cf. Landeskommission Berlin gegen Gewalt (2007), p. 193

Also sensible is that also judges get intercultural training so that they could better understand the situations and behaviour of foreign criminals. [23]

In addition actions concerning the legal status of foreigners should be done. For example should foreigners who have been staying in Germany for a long time be allowed to work although they only permissions to stay. It should also be possible for refugees and other foreigners to serve apprenticeships and to receive monetary support if they are in training among others e.g. according to the German "BaföG" (Berufsausbildungsförderungsgesetz).[24]

A broad educational background is one thing but the real prospect for a job is another thing. To improve transition from school to apprenticeship or work it would make sense if there would be a closer cooperation between schools, companies and the state. Besides also employees in the public job agencies should get intercultural trainings so that they can better understand the foreign mentality and give better advice. To sum up it is better for the state to help young foreigners getting into work and therefore to reduce crime than to make public transfer payments. [25]

Furthermore the task force recommends migrant organisations to take more responsibility, to do more public relations regarding ostracizing of violence (also within families), to discuss unpleasant but relevant topics as well as to provide better support for parents in upbringing their children. Moreover there should be more offices and own migrant organisations for Lebanese, Palestinian and former Yugoslavian people so that there is also a better representation of their interests. [26]

4. A process of rethinking instead of more severe punishment

Nowadays violent crimes committed by young men with foreign origins are a serious issue for the larger multicultural cities of the Federal Republic of Germany which absolutely need to be solved or at least considerably improved.

One suggestion to get an improvement in the situation was stated by Roland Koch (politician of the German Christian Democratic Party) during the election campaign in the Bundesland/ Federal State Hessen. According to his statement young criminals, so particularly young men with migrant backgrounds, should be severer punished and it should be easier to deport them from Germany. These legal changes could massively reduce the youth crime rate for the present but not for the future. It would merely mean to ease the effects on the society but not to examine and discuss the causes of their behavior as well as opportunities to improve their situations. It is anyway also not possible to send all young criminals into prison so more severe penalties could only act as a deterrent for them not to commit crimes and would therefore not really be a resolution to the problem.

Violent behavior might be in some cultural/ religious communities a legitimated and common way of carrying through one's will but it is in this case more likely an expression of being dissatisfied, frustrated and hopeless with no prospect for a positive change. Therefore the recommendations of the between 2005 to 2007 by the "Landeskommission Berlin gegen Gewalt" assigned task force are completely different to the suggestion of Roland Koch. It is not accurate only to hold foreign

---

[23] cf. Landeskommission Berlin gegen Gewalt (2007), p. 194-195
[24] cf. Landeskommission Berlin gegen Gewalt (2007), p. 200-205
[25] cf. Landeskommission Berlin gegen Gewalt (2007), p. 166-167
[26] cf. Landeskommission Berlin gegen Gewalt (2007), p. 196-199

families responsible for their bad social and economical situations as well as the violent crimes committed by their children. Also the German governments missed to attach enough significance to the adequate integration of foreigners from the beginning and there might still exist a structural discrimination of them by the society. A lot of foreigners live now and will probably in the future live in Germany and it is impossible to take no account of them. Therefore it would be good to initiate a process of rethinking by all participants to come from a differentiating feeling of We and They to a uniting feeling of We. The result of this could be that foreigners act non-violent and in accordance to the German law system as well as to make the biggest possible effort to learn the language, to get educated and therefore to get into work. Likewise should the German government grant them similar legal rights as Germans and bring down the structural discrimination so that they can find complete expression, can participate and consequently integrate into society. In the end also young men could retrieve the right path in life and a peaceful way to live in a society which holds all doors open for them. The conversion of legal and social actions has still been started with the German "Zuwanderungsgesetz" (2005), "Allgemeines Gleichbehandlungsgesetz" (2006) as well as the concepts of the Senate of Berlin "Vielfalt fördern – Zusammenhalt stärken" and "Integration durch Bildung". Now it is time for foreigners to show that they really want to integrate into and live peacefully in this society. The future development should be attentively followed. [27] [28] [29] [30]

---

[27] cf. Landeskommission Berlin gegen Gewalt (2007), p. 16-18
[28] cf. Landeskommission Berlin gegen Gewalt (2007), p. 58-62
[29] cf. Landeskommission Berlin gegen Gewalt (2007), p. 166-167
[30] cf. Landeskommission Berlin gegen Gewalt (2007), p. 200-206

Sources

Landeskommission Berlin gegen Gewalt (2007),
Berliner Forum Gewaltprävention Nr. 28, Gewalt von Jungen, männlichen
Jugendlichen und jungen Männern mit Migrationshintergrund in Berlin

Spiegel Online (2008a),
Teevs, Ch. / Volkery, C. , Kochs Wahlkampf kommt auf Touren, 02.02.2008, on
the internet: http://www.spiegel.de/politik/deutschland/0,1518,526239,00.html
[24.02.2008]

Spiegel Online (2008b),
Früher wegsperren, schneller abschieben, härter bestrafen, 02.01.2008, on the
internet: http://www.spiegel.de/politik/deutschland/0,1518,526271,00.html
[24.02.2008]

Süddeutsche (2007),
Schäfer, Ch. , Folgen eines Brandbriefes, 30.03.2007, on the internet:
URL: http://www.sueddeutsche.de/deutschland/artikel/956/107849/ [24.02.2008]

YOUR KNOWLEDGE HAS VALUE

- We will publish your bachelor's and master's thesis, essays and papers

- Your own eBook and book - sold worldwide in all relevant shops

- Earn money with each sale

Upload your text at www.GRIN.com and publish for free